Roadmap to God's Kingdom

Eleazar Marcelo

TEACH Services, Inc.
www.TEACHServices.com

**PRINTED IN
THE UNITED STATES OF AMERICA**

_____

Copyright © 2010 TEACH Services, Inc.
ISBN-13: 978-1-57258-634-5
Library of Congress Control Number: 201932375

Published by
TEACH Services, Inc.
www.TEACHServices.com

Contents

Preface

This book takes readers on a journey through the highway of time, illustrating the spectacular events foretold in prophecy from here to God's kingdom and beyond. We will let the Bible speak for itself. We will see the return of Jesus Christ, the mark of the beast, and Armageddon. We will climb the heights of Pisgah's mountain and from there we will view . . . eternity.

Preaching the Gospel

"And this gospel of the kingdom shall be preached in all the world as a witness unto all nations; and then shall the end come" (Matt. 24:14). This end-time message gives us a two-fold meaning. The gospel of the kingdom must first be preached in all the world, as a testimony to God's love and enduring mercy, and then shall the end come.

There is definitely an end to this world. In fact, the disciples asked the same question in verse 3 of the same chapter: "Tell us, when shall these things be? and what shall be the sign of thy coming, and of the end of the world?" The return of our Lord and Savior, Jesus Christ, is synonymous with the end of the world. But first, let us address the gospel message. What is it?

Throughout the ages of time, God has appointed people to proclaim the message of salvation to this sinful world. In the days of the antediluvians, Noah found grace in the eyes of the Lord and was chosen to carry out this task (Gen. 6:8). He was the messenger for his time.

The prophet Jonah was also called by the Lord to do His work: "Now the word of the LORD came unto Jonah the son of Amittai, saying, Arise, go to Nineveh, that great city, and cry against it; for their wickedness is come up before me" (Jonah 1:1, 2).

The Lord called him again a second time: "And the word of the LORD came unto Jonah the second time, saying, Arise, go unto Nineveh, that great city, and preach unto it the preaching that I bid thee" (Jonah 3:1, 2). This time he listened and obeyed. He entered into the city and proclaimed, "Yet forty days, and Nineveh shall be overthrown" (verse 4).

This was the message of salvation given to the people of Ninevah, and forty days was the timeframe from a merciful God. The people believed and proclaimed a fast. They covered themselves with sackcloth, turned from their evil ways, and repented of their evil deeds (verses 5-8).

> Throughout the ages of time, God has appointed people to proclaim the message of salvation to this sinful world.

"And God saw their works, that they turned from their evil way; and God repented of the evil, that he had said that he would do unto them; and he did it not" (verse 10). The people of Nineveh were saved from the wrath of a merciful, gracious, and loving God.

Turning to Ezekiel, we read about the Lord God calling the Israelites to repentance: "Repent, and turn yourselves from all your transgressions; so iniquity shall not be your ruin. Cast away from you all your transgressions, whereby ye have transgressed; and make you a new heart and a new spirit: for why will ye die, O house of Israel? For I have no pleasure in the death of him that dieth, saith the Lord GOD: wherefore turn yourselves, and live ye" (18:30-32).

In the days of the apostles, they preached the same message of salvation. They did not have microphones, loudspeakers, or electronics of any sort. Yet, Peter preached and said unto them, "Repent, and be baptized every one of you in the name of Jesus Christ for the remission of sins, and ye shall receive the gift of the Holy Ghost. . . . Then they that gladly received his word were baptized: and the same day there were added unto them about three thousand souls" (Acts 2:38, 41).

While the wages of sin is death (Rom. 6:23), repentance is the common denominator in all these passages, and it is the key to forgiveness. If there is no repentance, there is no remission of sins, and if there is no remission of sins, there is also no forgiveness.

"And I saw another angel fly in the midst of heaven, having the everlasting gospel to preach unto them that dwell on the earth, and to every nation, and kindred, and tongue, and people" (Rev. 14:6). The gospel message is said to be "everlasting" because its message remains the same for this sinful world. In the Old Testament times, the message was about repentance. In the New Testament, the message is still about repentance: "The Lord is . . . not willing that any should perish, but that all should come to repentance" (2 Peter 3:9).

Let us not forget Jesus' commission to all believers: "Go ye therefore, and teach all nations, baptizing them in the name of the Father, and of the Son, and of the Holy Ghost: Teaching them to observe all things whatsoever I have commanded you: and, lo, I am with you always, even unto the end of the world" (Matt. 28:19, 20).

3

He tells us to beware for "they will deliver you up to the councils, and they will scourge you in their synagogues; And ye shall be brought before governors and kings for my sake . . . But when they deliver you up, take no thought how or what ye shall speak: for it shall be given you in that same hour what ye shall speak. For it is not ye that speak, but the Spirit of your Father which speaketh in you. And the brother shall deliver up the brother to death, and the father the child: and the children shall rise up against their parents, and cause them to be put to death. And ye shall be hated of all men for my name's sake: but he that endureth to the end shall be saved" (Matt. 10:17-22).

Jesus' promise that He is with us always, "even unto the end of the world," is the greatest assurance in the work of preaching the gospel. He stands behind His work and all those whom He sends as sheep in the midst of wolves, delivering the message of hope to this dying world. He has the power to help us accomplish this goal (Matt. 28:18).

The Lord loves us dearly. He wants us to be sanctified and ready for the judgment day.

Judgment On-Going, Court in Session

In Revelation 14:7, John wrote, "Saying with a loud voice, Fear God, and give glory to him; for the hour of his judgment is come: and worship him that made heaven, and earth, and the sea, and the fountains of waters."

"Fear God and give glory to Him for the hour of His judgment is come" is the urgent message given here. There is a judgment and the hour of this judgment has come, according to John. We are called to worship Him that made heaven and earth, not that which He has created.

"I beheld till the thrones were cast down, and the Ancient of days did sit, whose garment was white as snow, and the hair of his head like the pure wool: his throne was like the fiery flame, and his wheels as burning fire. A fiery stream issued and came forth from before him: thousand thousands ministered unto him, and ten thousand times ten thousand stood before him: the judgment was set, and the books were opened" (Daniel 7:9, 10).

Roadmap to God's Kingdom

The "ancient of days" is the Son of God. He is the judge (John 5:22, 27). He has been around since the beginning of time. The "garment white as snow" represents perfection (robe of righteousness), which only Jesus Christ, the Savior of the world, could wear as He sits on the judgment throne. "Thousand thousands ministered unto him" represents the heavenly host of angels assisting him. "Ten thousand times ten thousand stood before him" is symbolic of all who will be judged, and everyone will be judged—"the judgment was set, and the books were opened." The heavenly court is in session.

A vision given to John about the same judgment is recorded in Revelation 20:12: "And I saw the dead, small and great, stand before God; and the books were opened; and another book was opened, which is the book of life: and the dead were judged out of those things which were written in the books, according to their works."

The dead will not be resurrected to stand before God in the judgment hall. They will remain dead. Their names will stand for them when called and the records of their deeds in the heavenly books will witness for them. However, the righteous will be resurrected when Jesus comes (I Thess. 4: 16), and after a thousand years, there will be a second resurrection. This time it will be for the wicked (Rev. 20:5).

To prepare for the judgment, we must "fear God, and keep his commandments: for this is the whole duty of man" (Eccl. 12:13). Jesus says in John 14:15, "If ye love me, keep my commandments." John also wrote, "He that saith, I know him, and keepeth not his commandments, is a liar, and the truth is not in him" (1 John 2:4). When we transgress one of His words or laws, we sin and that sin is recorded in the heavenly books. This is sin by transgression (1 John 3:4).

If, however, we confess and repent of that sin, that same sin is forgiven and marked as such. This process begins at birth (spiritual birth) or baptism and continues throughout our life. We fall; we rise. It is called the process of sanctification. It would be nice if, after we are baptized, we no longer sinned. However, as long as we are in this mortal and sinful body, we will tend to sin. But, as long as we stay on the side of righteousness through confession and repentance and overcoming temptation, by the grace of God, our names will stay in the book of life in heaven (Rev. 3:5).

Jesus Christ, the judge, will be thorough on judgment day: "For God shall bring every work into judgment, with every secret thing, whether it be good, or whether it be

> Jesus says in John 14:15, "If ye love me, keep my commandments."

evil" (Eccl. 12:14). This part of the judgment is called the "investigative" or trial phase. This is the time when our individual cases are tried, when our "book of life" in heaven is opened and examined (Rev. 20:12).

Who will be judged? The apostle Paul tells us in 2 Corinthians 5:10, "For we must all appear before the judgment seat of Christ; that every one may receive the things done in his body, according to that he hath done, whether it be good or bad." We will all be judged. One by one we will be judged according to "the things done in his body." God created us "in his own image, in the image of God created he him; male and female created he them" (Gen. 1:27). He expects us to be the same way when He returns.

Are we going to be judged as individuals? Revelation 20:13 says, "And they were judged every man according to their works." Just like with our salvation in which we must "work out [our] own salvation with fear and trembling" (Phil. 2:12), we will be judged individually. We will not be judged nor saved as a church.

> Everyone is in for his reward when Jesus Christ returns . . .

Where is the judgment hall? The judgment hall is in a more perfect tabernacle not made with hands. It is in heaven where the book of life is kept. "For Christ is not entered into holy places made with hands, which are figures of the true; but into heaven itself, now to appear in the presence of God for us" (Heb. 9:24).

Will I know when the trial phase is over? When the trial phase of the judgment ends, "He that is unjust, let him be unjust still: and he which is filthy, let him be filthy still: and he that is righteous, let him be righteous still: and he that is holy, let him be holy still" (Rev. 22:11).

Wherever your heart and mind is set at the close of the judgment, you will be there for good. No more changing your mind. Decisions will be final. Everyone is in for his reward when Jesus Christ returns: some for eternal life, some for eternal damnation. "For the Son of man shall come in the glory of his Father, with his angels; and then he shall reward every man according to his works" (Matt. 16:27).

Lest we forget God's commandments and His call to obey them, following are the Ten Commandments as written by God in Exodus 20:3-17:

1.   Thou shalt have no other gods before me.

2. Thou shalt not make unto thee any graven image, or any likeness of any thing that is in heaven above, or that is in the earth beneath, or that is in the water under the earth. Thou shalt not bow down thyself to them, nor serve them: for I the LORD thy God am a jealous God, visiting the iniquity of the fathers upon the children unto the third and fourth generation of them that hate me. And shewing mercy unto thousands of them that love me, and keep my commandments.

3. Thou shalt not take the name of the LORD thy God in vain; for the LORD will not hold him guiltless that taketh his name in vain.

4. Remember the sabbath day to keep it holy. Six days shalt thou labour, and do all thy work: But the seventh day is the sabbath of the LORD thy God: in it thou shalt not do any work, thou, nor thy son, nor thy daughter, thy manservant, nor thy maidservant, nor thy cattle, nor thy stranger that is within thy gates: For in six days the LORD made heaven and earth, the sea, and all that is in them is, and rested the seventh day: wherefore the LORD blessed the sabbath day, and hallowed it.

5. Honour thy father and thy mother: that thy days may be long upon the land which the LORD thy God giveth thee.

6. Thou shalt not kill.

7. Thou shalt not commit adultery.

8. Thou shalt not steal.

9. Thou shalt not bear false witness against thy neighbour.

10. Thou shalt not covet thy neighbour's house, thou shalt not covet thy neighbour's wife, nor his manservant, nor his maidservant, nor his ox, nor his ass, nor any thing that is thy neighbour's.

9

The Sheep and The Goat

"When the Son of man shall come in his glory, and all the holy angels with him, then shall he sit upon the throne of his glory: And before him shall be gathered all nations: and he shall separate them one from another, as a shepherd divideth his sheep from the goats" (Matt. 25:31, 32). Sound familiar? This is symbolic of the same judgment from another view. Continuing in verse 33, "And he shall set the sheep on his right hand, but the goats on the left."

Now, take note of the following verse: "Then shall the King say unto them on his right hand, Come, ye blessed of my Father, inherit the kingdom prepared for you from the foundation of the world" (verse 34).

The Lord does not decide who will be the sheep and who will be the goats. The sheep choose to be sheep by virtue of the life they live on this earth as recorded in the books above, and in the same token, the goats make a similar choice. If the Lord finds you to be a sheep on judgment day, He will set you on his right hand. If He finds you to be a goat, He will set you on His left.

We all have to make our own decision as to where we want to spend eternity by proving to God who we are at the time of judgment. God does not force anyone to follow Him. We all were given the same freedom to choose whom we want to serve: God or mammon (Matt. 6:24). We cannot serve two masters at the same time. We serve only one. We cannot be in love with the things of this world and be in love with God at the same time.

How does this separation of the sheep from the goats actually transform in real life today? There are two main gates mentioned in the New Testament for us to read about and understand. "Enter ye in at the strait gate: for wide is the gate, and broad is the way, that leadeth to destruction, and many there be that go in thereat: Because strait is the gate, and narrow is the way, which leadeth unto life, and few there be that find it" (Matt. 7:13, 14). Let us understand this carefully and see what God is telling us, because these are gates that will lead either to heaven or to hell.

> We cannot be in love with the things of this world and be in love with God at the same time.

The first gate is wide, and the way is broad. Many enter this gate. Where does this lead to? Destruction. In other words, hell. Now, the second gate is straight, "and narrow is the way, which leadeth unto life, and few there be that find it." What are the adjectives used to differentiate one gate from the other? "Many" for the wide gate, and "few" for the straight. The term "strait" reminds me of a man pulled over by a highway patrol officer for possible intoxication. He was asked to walk a straight line. If he wavers, he goes to jail. If not, he is good and free to move on.

11

The word "narrow" denotes "discipline" in our spiritual life. This is where all the "thou shalt nots" come in—Thou shalt not kill; thou shalt not steal; thou shalt not commit adultery. Despite all these restrictions God gave, it is still much easier to follow and obey the Ten Commandments of God than to disobey them. Isn't it better to stay home in the warmth of your living room than to rob a bank? It takes time and effort to get involved in such a risky business. It may even cost you your life. It is "work" to disobey the law of God.

By the way, there is more to the ten principles embodied in the Ten Commandments of God. For example, Satan was not cast down to this earth from heaven because he murdered someone, stole money, or perhaps committed adultery. He did something far worse while he was in heaven: "I will exalt my throne above the stars of God: I will sit also upon the mount of the congregation . . .

> To know and understand what humble means and to live it in preparation for the kingdom of God, we must remember what Jesus said . . .

. I will ascend above the heights of the clouds; I will be like the most High" (Isa. 14:13, 14). Satan became proud of himself and this is why he was cast down to earth.

Pride is a common sin we tend to overlook, and it is a sin that will bar us from entering the kingdom of God. It is there; it is left unnoticed and unchecked. It is almost inherent and prevalent in the lives of many. It ranges from early childhood to even the most seasoned individual. You see it in the marketplace, in educational institutions, and even in churches. I love people in politics, but one cannot be a politician without having to prove himself, his accomplishments, and how good he is. This is the opposite of meek-

12

ness. It would be nice if one could just humble himself, uplift his opponent, and still win the election. But that is asking too much.

To know and understand what humble means and to live it in preparation for the kingdom of God, we must remember what Jesus said: "Take my yoke upon you, and learn of me; for I am meek and lowly in heart: and ye shall find rest unto your souls" (Matt. 11:29). Heaven has no place for the proud and rebellious. It is all about humility and obedience.

The Wide Gate and Broad Way

In this gate, spiritual Babylon will form. They will form in the name of love, peace, and unity. It is a very powerful name. Although it means confusion, it also symbolizes supremacy. As John said, "And I saw three unclean spirits like frogs come out of the mouth of the dragon, and out of the mouth of the beast, and out of the mouth of the false prophet" (Rev. 16:13). The false prophets are those who profess to follow Christ but end up joining with the beast and his followers.

The dragon, the beast, and the false prophets will perform miracles and go forth unto the kings of the earth to prepare to gather them to the battle of that great day of God, and this "wide gate" will be the gathering place. The greatest miracle the "three unclean spirits" will do is unite the whole world into one solid Babylon, headed by the beast. It will be the greatest miracle because these multiple faiths are extremely different from one another in doctrinal issues and practices. Yet, they will join one another.

Many different faiths will gather here because it is here where they have modem form of worships. They ordain women and form "praise teams" composed of youth to sing contemporary songs. Some use drums and guitars, some don't. But they clap their hands while moving their bodies to the tune. It is entertaining. It excites the senses. It is the key used to join all these faiths together to form one unified Babylon. Some of God's people are here today, and they will stay until they hear the call from God to come out.

Revelation 14:8 tells us, "And there followed another angel, saying, Babylon is fallen, is fallen, that great city, because she made all nations drink of the wine of the wrath of her fornication." The term used here as "fallen" refers to her spiritual condition. She has fallen, because she has indoctrinated the world with her image (Sunday observance) and apostate beliefs. She is huge in number and great in religious, economic, and political power, but she no longer demonstrates her vigor in faith and piety.

> Though Babylon is still segregated by some barriers today, she stands as a worldwide movement, silently compelling the world to unite.

Though Babylon is still segregated by some barriers today, she stands as a worldwide movement, silently compelling the world to unite. And the world will unite under her banner because the Bible says so: "Then shall ye [Jesus Christ] return, and discern between the righteous and the wicked, between him that serveth God and him that serveth him not" (Mal. 3:18).

Let us visit the other gate.

The Strait Gate and Narrow Way

"Because strait is the gate and narrow is the way, which leadeth unto life, and few there be that find it" (Matt. 7:13, 14). In this gate, as we have mentioned earlier, there are many restrictions. There are many "thou shalt nots." Don't drink, don't smoke, don't do this, don't eat that! People who walk through this gate follow what the Lord said to be clean and unclean in foods. They do not eat swine, crabs, lobsters, and the like (Lev. 11). They live simple lives (1 Tim. 6:7, 8). The narrow way is not popular, and although God wants everyone to be here, it is just not the choice for most people.

These are God's saints. They are the wheat. They are here, but they are not alone. The tares are here too, worshipping with them. But that is okay because God says that the wheat and the tares must grow together until the harvest comes (Matt. 13:30). They are here with the saints and because they outnumber them, they are the ones leading the church. This is the reason why God gave this group another name.

It is called Laodicea (Rev. 3:14-19). They are neither cold nor hot. They are lukewarm. They think they are rich and increased with goods and have need of nothing. What they do not know is that they are wretched, miserable, poor, blind, and naked. God tells them to buy of him "gold tried in the fire," that they may be rich, white raiment that they may be clothed, so the shame of their nakedness does not show, and eyesalve that they may see who they are. God rebukes and chastens them because He loves them. He wants them back. He tells them to be zealous and repent. Will the church of Laodicea remain in existence, without the Laodiceans leading?

> Heaven is all about perfection and the willingness to obey.

What is interesting about these two groups in the two gates is that they both attest to keep the law of God. They both agree not to kill. They both agree not to steal. They both agree not to commit adultery, etc.; but when it comes to the fourth commandment, which is the seventh-day Sabbath of the Lord thy God, they differ in opinion and practice of faith. That is why they separate. In James 2:10 it says, "For whosoever shall keep the whole law, and yet offend in one point, he is guilty of all."

We cannot just keep nine of its precepts and ignore the fourth. "Be ye therefore perfect, even as your Father which is in heaven is perfect" (Matt. 5:48). Heaven is all about perfection and the willingness to obey.

17

America in Prophecy

"And I beheld another beast coming up out of the earth; and he had two horns like a lamb, and he spake as a dragon" (Rev. 13:11). The United States of America is said to be the country in the world to fulfill this prophecy—to compel everyone to observe Sunday as the Lord's day regardless of one's faith and personal conviction. The U.S. is likened to a lamb, gentle and innocent, but it is capable of getting things done when it speaks: "And he exerciseth all the power of the first beast before him, and causeth the earth and them which dwell therein to worship the first beast, whose deadly wound was healed" (verse 12).

The first beast mentioned here changed the day of the Lord from the seventh day of the week to the first day of the week, which majority of Christian churches now observe. What is the seventh day according to the Bible, the calendar, and Webster's dictionary? "The seventh day is the sabbath of the Lord thy God" (Ex. 20:10). The calendar lists Saturday as the seventh day of the week, and Webster's dictionary mentions that Saturday is observed as the Sabbath by the Jews and other Christians.

The Jews of today are descendants of the Jews we read about during the time of Christ. This is why they worship God on the Sabbath day. Jesus Christ was also a Jew, but that is not the reason why He wants us to observe it. After creating the heavens and the earth in six days, He rested on the seventh day, blessed it, and sanctified it (Gen. 2:1-3). No other day of the week was blessed by God and made holy, except the seventh day, which is the Sabbath.

The apostles also observed the Sabbath and worshipped God on this day. In Acts 13:42-44 it says, "And when the Jews were gone out of the synagogue, the Gentiles besought that these words might be preached to them the next sabbath. Now when the congregation was broken up, many of the Jews and religious proselytes followed Paul and Barnabas: who, speaking to

> No other day of the week was blessed by God and made holy, except the seventh day, which is the Sabbath.

them, persuaded them to continue in the grace of God. And the next sabbath day came almost the whole city together to hear the word of God." In this passage, we confirm that Paul and Barnabas and the Jews and the Gentiles were all Sabbath keepers.

Turning over a few chapters, we will look at Acts 20:7. For the purpose of understanding this text, it is good to know that God divides the day from sundown to sundown (Gen. 1). "And upon the first day of the week, when the disciples came together to break bread, Paul preached unto them, ready to depart on the morrow; and continued his speech until midnight." Paul did not preach on the first day of the week. It reads and "upon" the first day of the week. It does not read "and on the first day" of the week, does it? "Upon" is used here as approaching the first day. It was still Sabbath, or Saturday. It was not sundown yet.

19

It is interesting that the word "Sabbath" is observed by two groups of Christians—one on the seventh day as the Bible states, and one on the first day of the week. The seventh-day Sabbath is from God. The Sunday Sabbath is from the beast. Webster's dictionary further states that "Sabbath Sunday" is the first day of the week, which is observed by most Christians. In the parable of the wide and straight gate, many and few, where are you? If Rome had not changed the Lord's day, all of the Christian world would still be keeping the seventh-day Sabbath. The Jews are the most tangible proof we have of the Sabbath history.

> When this happens, religious freedom and freedom of speech will disappear with all the other freedoms America once stood and fought for.

Is it surprising that the first beast of Revelation 13 changed the Sabbath of God, which is in the fourth commandment? No, it is not, because we were warned by God in Daniel 7:25 that these things will take place: "And he shall speak great words against the most High, and shall wear out the saints of the most High, and think to change times and laws: and they shall be given into his hand until a time and times and the dividing of time."

God's Sabbath was changed from the seventh day of the week, which is the fourth commandment, to the first day. "And he had power to give life unto the image of the beast, that the image of the beast should both speak, and cause that as many as would not worship the image of the beast should be killed" (Rev. 13:15). Since the beast changed the Lord's day and has been widely observed throughout the world, that same change, "Sunday keeping," has become his image as the Bible points out. This change did not happen without a price to the lives of thousands and thousands of

20

Christians throughout the world: "And I saw the woman [apostate church] drunken with the blood of the saints, and with the blood of the martyrs of Jesus" (Rev. 17:6).

This is what "and shall wear out the saints" means in the words of Daniel. This prophecy was fulfilled after the first "Sunday law" was decreed by Constantine the Great, in Rome, in AD 321. They say history repeats itself. This will become true when America legislates another "Sunday law." When this happens, religious freedom and freedom of speech will disappear with all the other freedoms America once stood and fought for. She will order, through her courts, every citizen to worship on Sunday under the penalty of death. "And cause that as many as would not worship the image of the beast should be killed." Then, history will repeat itself.

John said, "And I saw the souls of them that were beheaded for the witness of Jesus, and for the word of God, and which had not worshipped the beast, neither his image, neither had received his mark upon their foreheads, or in their hands" (Rev. 20:4). "And I saw the woman [church] drunken with the blood of the saints, and with the blood of the martyrs of Jesus" (Rev. 17:6).

The prophet Daniel puts it bluntly in these words: "And at that time shall Michael stand up, the great prince which standeth for the children of thy people: and there shall be a time of trouble, such as never was since there was a nation even to that same time: and at that time thy people shall be delivered, every one that shall be found written in the book" (Dan. 12:1). This is the "book of life" we referred to.

The physician Luke says, "But before all these, they shall lay their hands on you, and persecute you, delivering you up to the synagogues, and into prisons, being brought before kings and rulers for my name's sake. . . . And ye shall be betrayed both by parents, and bretheren, and kinsfolks, and friends; and some of you shall they cause to be put to death" (Luke 21:12, 16).

We are warned about the coming trials: "For then shall be great tribulation, such as was not since the beginning of the world to this time, no, nor ever shall be. And except those days should be shortened, there should no flesh be saved: but for the elect's sake those days shall be shortened" (Matt. 24:21, 22).

The Sunday law will come in two phases. The first will be introductory in nature. The second will be strictly mandatory with orders to kill everyone who will not adhere to the law or who are deemed a "heretic." Thus fulfills the latter part of the verse: "And cause that as many as would not worship the image of the beast should be killed" (Rev. 13:15).

The observance of Sunday has lost its strength under the freedom of religion we enjoy today compared to the era of the dark ages. Anyone can observe any day of the week without the government intervening. America, exercising all the power of the first beast, will revive the observance of Sunday worship for all by enacting a second blue "Sunday law." Then everyone will be compelled to observe it. Today, the Jews and some Christians are still in obedience with God's seventh-day Sabbath.

The Early and Latter Rain

"And it shall come to pass in the last days, saith God, I will pour out my Spirit upon all flesh: and your sons and your daughters shall prophesy, and your young men shall see visions, and your old men shall dream dreams" (Acts 2:17). If we believe we are in the last days, this message about the pouring out of the Holy Spirit is clearly for us. It is the "latter rain." God is waiting to pour it out, and He will, as soon as we are ready.

God poured out His Spirit on the early church: "And suddenly there came a sound from heaven as of a rushing mighty wind, and it filled all the house where they were sitting. And there appeared unto them cloven tongues like as of fire, and it sat upon each of them. And they were all filled with the Holy Ghost, and began to speak with other tongues, as the Spirit gave them utterance" (verses 2-4). The Holy Spirit came unto them like a rushing mighty wind, and it filled all the house where they were sitting. The twelve apostles experienced the outpouring of the Holy Spirit. We will, too! Let us examine their spiritual condition when it happened.

"And when the days of Pentecost was fully come, they were all with one accord in one place" (verse 1). They were all in one accord, and they were all together in one place. That was the key, and it tells a lot. It tells us that the apostles were unified in one mind and spirit. There were no disagreements and no dissention. If there were some, they were laid aside in the spirit of love and forgiveness. Faults were confessed with one another, and the Spirit of God moved in their hearts. They were bonded together. They went from house to house, broke bread, and ate their meat with gladness and singleness of heart. The Lord added to the church daily such as should be saved (verse 46, 47).

> God is willing and ready to pour out the latter rain to His church, but they have to unite to His side in one accord.

It was the pioneering days of Christianity. The apostles planted the seeds of the gospel, and God gave them the much-needed rain, the "early rain" of the Holy Spirit to propagate their work. They went from place to place preaching the message of salvation, baptizing them in the name of the Father, and of the Son, and of the Holy Spirit. The outpouring of the Holy Ghost on the day of Pentecost led them to baptize three thousand souls in one day. That was awesome.

That was awesome because those three thousand souls were of different nations and languages. They were From Parthians, Medes, Elam, Mesopotamia, Judaea, Cappadocia, Pontus, and Asia. They were from Phrygia, Pamphylia, Egypt, Libya, Cyrene, and Rome. There were Cretes and Arabians, too. Peter preached and said unto them, Repent and be baptized every one of you in the name of Jesus Christ for the remission of sins and you shall receive the gift of the Holy Ghost; they received it as he said. They

24

heard and understood every word of what Peter preached and they understood it clearly in their very own languages. That was the gift of tongue and that is how it works. It communicates the message from the speaker to the hearers even if they are of different nationalities (verses 4-11).

God is willing and ready to pour out the latter rain to His church, but they have to unite to His side in one accord. The rain is needed this time not for planting, but for the harvest. "The harvest truly is plenteous, but the labourers are few; Pray ye therefore the Lord of the harvest, that he will send forth labourers into his harvest" (Matt. 9:37, 38).

Once the people of God are sanctified, we will see the latter rain poured out upon the church, and there will be a harvest of souls not seen since the days of the apostles. "Your sons and your daughters shall prophesy, your old men shall dream dreams, your young men shall see visions" (Joel 2:28).

The Loud Cry

"And the third angel followed them, saying with a loud voice, If any man worship the beast and his image [adhering to the Sunday Sabbath], and receive his mark in his forehead, or in his hand, The same shall drink of the wine of the wrath of God, which is poured out without mixture into the cup of his indignation; and he shall be tormented with fire and brimstone [in hell at the end of time] in the presence of the holy angels, and in the presence of the Lamb: And the smoke of their torment ascendeth up for ever and ever: and they have no rest day nor night, who worship the beast and his image, and whosoever receiveth the mark of his name" (Rev. 14:9-11).

While the third angel gives us enough warning not to worship the beast and his image, John heard another voice from heaven: "And I heard another voice from heaven saying, come out of her, my people, that ye be not partakers of her sins, and that ye receive not of her plagues. For her sins have reached unto heaven, and God hath remembered her iniquities" (Rev. 18:4, 5).

The saints, empowered by the Holy Ghost through the latter rain, will call to God's people who are still in Babylon to come out before her judgment is given her. God's mercy and saving grace linger at this point. The Sunday law is at the pinnacle of enforcement and judgment has not closed. They will hear the voice of God calling them, and they will gladly come out to join the commandment-keeping people of God.

"Therefore shall her plagues come in one day [one day in prophecy is one literal year], death, and mourning, and famine; and she shall be utterly burned with fire: for strong is the Lord God who judgeth her. And the kings of the earth, who have committed fornication and lived deliciously with her, shall bewail her, and lament for her, when they shall see the smoke of her burning. Standing afar off for the fear of her torment, saying, Alas, alas that great city Babylon, that mighty city! for in one hour is thy judgment come" (Rev. 18:8-10). This is when her wealth comes into naught, turning into ashes.

> God's mercy and saving grace linger at this point.

"And they cast dust on their heads, and cried, weeping and wailing, saying, Alas, alas, that great city, wherein were made rich all that have ships in the sea by reason of her costliness! for in one hour is she made desolate" (verse 19). "Rejoice over her, thou heaven, and ye holy apostles and prophets; for God hath avenged you on her" (verse 20). "And in her was found the blood of prophets, and of saints, and of all that were slain upon the earth" (verse 24).

The One Hundred Forty Four Thousand Sealed

"And after these things I saw four angels standing on the four comers of the earth, holding the four winds of the earth, that the winds should not blow on the earth, nor on the sea, nor on any tree. And I saw another angel ascending from the east, having the seal of the living God: and he cried with a loud voice to the four angels, to whom it was given to hurt the earth and the sea, Saying, Hurt not the earth, neither the sea, nor the trees, till we have sealed the servants of our God in their foreheads. And I heard the number of them which were sealed: and there were sealed an hundred and forty and four thousand of all the tribes of the children of Israel" (Rev. 7:1-4).

The "one hundred and forty and four thousand" who were sealed by the angel is a symbolic number. It is not fixed. If this were a fixed, literal number of those who will be saved from the tribes of Israel, there is no need to preach the gospel of Christ to the world. There is no need to win souls. Reading the chapter all the way to verse 8 tells us that the one hundred forty four thousand is the sum of twelve thousand from each tribe times twelve tribes.

Now, why would God save twelve thousand from each tribe when most of these tribes apostatized? Twelve thousand from Judah, twelve thousand from Rueben, twelve thousand from Gad. The reason is, He demonstrates His fairness and justice to all of us. He tells us that salvation is equally given to everyone who comes to Him. And the word Israel here denotes "spiritual Israel." I am not a Jew. I am a Gentile, but I hope to be with the one hundred forty four thousand who will be saved when He comes.

As soon as the Sunday law is passed, the angel of Revelation 7 will start sealing those who have proven themselves loyal to the creator of heaven and earth by keeping His commandments. He will seal them one by one with the

> ## The Sunday law will be the final test given to the human race at the end of time.

seal of the living God until everyone who will be sealed is sealed. Then judgment to the world will end. Those who do not receive the "seal of the living God" will receive the "mark of the beast" (Rev. 13:1, 6-18).

The Sunday law will be the final test given to the human race at the end of time. Every soul will be confronted with this issue, everyone will be tested. It will be a test of loyalty. Whom do you serve, God or mammon? Those who serve God will receive the seal, and those who serve mammon will receive the 666 mark of the beast.

John said, "And I looked, and, lo, a Lamb stood on the mount Sion, and with him an hundred forty and four thousand, having his Father's name written in their foreheads. And I heard a voice from heaven, as the voice of many waters, and as the voice of a great thunder: and I heard the voice of harpers harping with their harps: And they sung as it were a new song before the throne, and before the four beasts, and the elders: and no man could learn that song but the hundred and forty and four thousand, which were redeemed from the earth. These are they which were not defiled with women; for they are virgins. These are they which follow the Lamb whithersoever he goeth. These were redeemed from among men, being the firstfruits unto God and to the Lamb. And in their mouth was found no guile: for they are without fault before the throne of God" (Rev. 14:1-5).

These saints were also sinners, but they confessed and repented of their transgressions against the law of God. They were repentant sinners sanctified by God. When they were tried at the judgment hall, they were found "without fault," forgiven. They were born in the commandment-keeping church of God. "They were not defiled by woman." They have not known nor accepted any of the apostate teachings "for they are virgins."

Judgment Has Ended,
the Court Adjourns

Judgment has ended. There is no more preaching of the gospel. No more exchanges from either camp. The two gates are closed. "He that is unjust, let him be unjust still: and he which is filthy, let him be filthy still: and he that is righteous, let him be righteous still: and he that is holy, let him be holy still" (Rev. 22:11). Every book has been reviewed. Every case has been settled. Everyone has been judged. The heavenly court has adjourned.

Here on earth, the saints of God are sealed. "These are they which came out of tribulation, and have washed their robes [have confessed and repented of their sins to God], and made them white in the blood of the Lamb" (Rev. 7:14). They are sealed with the seal of the living God and all those who worship the beast and his image receive the 666 mark, the mark of the beast (Rev. 13:16-18).

The Lord God sent His angel to tell John, "Seal not the sayings of the prophecy of this book: for the time is at hand" (Rev. 22:10). Indeed, the time is at hand. "And, behold, I come quickly;

and my reward is with me, to give every man according as his work shall be" (verse 12). It is a reward He brings with Him when He comes. The trial phase has ended. Judgment is over. This is now the sentencing period. The sentence is either "life eternal" for the righteous or "eternal damnation in hell" for the wicked.

> The Lord God sent His angel to tell John, "Seal not the sayings of the prophecy of this book: for the time is at hand" (Rev. 22:10).

Here are those who have chosen to enter the "strait gate and narrow way." They have passed the deceptive snare of the devil and the pressure to "worship the image of the beast." It was their strong faith in God that brought them thus far. They are victorious. They have proven their allegiance to the creator of heaven and earth and are sealed with the "seal of the living God." Although they have passed the judgment, they are yet to be redeemed by Jesus Christ their Savior. While waiting for their redemption, they will face the most severe test of all—the 'time of trouble.

Time of Trouble for
the Saints of God

The period of leniency on the part of the beast is over. The Sunday law has now come to the second phase—a death decree for the saints of God. The image of the beast—the Sunday law—now serves as an instrument to kill the saints for keeping the commandments of God. "And cause that as many as would not worship the image of the beast should be killed" (Rev. 13:15). This is the time when history will repeat itself. It happened in the reign of the first beast (verse 7), and it will happen again in the prophecy of America.

This is the vision that was shown to the prophet Daniel "And there shall be a time of trouble, such as never was since there was a nation" (Dan. 12:1). The same vision was also shown to John in Revelation 12:17: "And the dragon was wroth with the woman [woman in Bible prophecy represents a church], and went to make war with the remnant of her seed, which keep the commandments of God, and have the testimony of Jesus Christ."

The devil, wroth with the woman, will not go alone to make war with the church that keeps the commandments of God—"the remnant of her seed." The devil employs the beast and the false prophets. This is a part of the progressive action of the "three unclean spirits" that eventually will go to the kings of the earth to gather them to the battle of that great day of God Almighty (Rev. 16:13, 14).

> The devil, wroth with the woman, will not go alone to make war with the church that keeps the commandments of God—"the remnant of her seed."

There is a church that keeps the commandments of God and has the testimony of Jesus Christ (Rev. 14:12)—"the testimony of Jesus is the spirit of prophecy" (Rev. 19:10). They have the gift of prophecy and are found all over the world, preaching the message of salvation while preparing themselves for His soon appearing.

This time, the commandment-keeping church has greatly reduced in number. They are down to the "remnant of her seed," and the Scripture describes them now as the remnant church (Rom. 9:27). The latter rain of the Holy Spirit was poured out by God in good measure, causing them to revive and be on fire. The Laodiceans were sanctified and those who would not were shaken out to Babylon. They have returned to the old-fashion way of "traditional worship," sacred and solemn. One can feel the presence of God. They do not question Him on why He chose to ordain only the men. They focus their eyes on Him in awe and abide by His decision. They don't clap their hands as they do in public arenas or stadiums. They know they are in the house of God and the house of God is holy.

There is no modem, contemporary, swinging modes in music. They sing their hymns to Him in the beauty of holiness. No one wears jewelry, not even wedding bands (Isa. 3:16-26). They live simple lives. They are the "peculiar" people of God (1 Peter 2:9). Their peculiarity reveals so much that if they mingle in the midst of a huge congregation, they can be distinctly recognized. This is the same church the devil is wroth about that he will persecute and try to kill—"the remnant of her seed, which keep the commandments of God" (Rev. 12:17).

The beast is in power. It is the controlling power of the devil. It controls and directs the entire movement of persecuting God's remnant people. It has an army of ministers, apostles, and deceitful workers who transform themselves into the apostles of Christ (2 Cor. 11:13-15). They counterfeit every work and example that Jesus Christ has laid out for us. They change them and they are changed, not without a reason. They do such an excellent job that many people are deceived—"That old serpent, called the Devil, and Satan, which deceiveth the whole world" (Rev. 12:9). Those whom he will have deceived at the end of time is best described as the "sands of the sea" (Rev. 20:8).

Jesus reminds us in Matthew 5:11, 12 that we should rejoice in the midst of persecution: "Blessed are ye, when men shall revile you, and persecute you, and shall say all manner of evil against you falsely, for my sake. Rejoice, and be exceeding glad: for great is your reward in heaven: for so persecuted they the prophets which were before you." These were the comforting words of Jesus to all of His apostles.

Let's now look at Matthew 24:15-21: "When ye therefore shall see the abomination of desolation, spoken of by Daniel the prophet, stand in the holy place" (verse 15). Those who are in

Judea, flee to the mountains. Do not take anything out of your house and those who are in the fields, do not go home to take your clothes. And woe unto them who are with young child that are not weaned. Pray that your flight be not in the winter, nor on the Sabbath day. "For then shall be the great tribulation, such as was not since the beginning of the world to this time, no, nor ever shall be" (verse 21).

> Jesus reminds us in Matthew 5:11, 12 that we should rejoice in the midst of persecution.

The saints of God will be greatly tested. They will not be able to buy food anymore. "And that no man might buy or sell, save he that had the mark, or the name of the beast, or the number of his name" (Rev. 13:17). They will be on the run. They will hide whenever and wherever they can, but "he that shall endure unto the end, the same shall be saved" (Matt. 24:13). That is the promise—it is their hope. "Here is the patience of the saints: here are they that keep the commandments of God, and the faith of Jesus" (Rev. 14:12).

Will God forsake His very own?

The Seven Last Plagues Poured

We will now review Revelation 16: "And I heard a great voice out of the temple saying to the seven angels, Go your ways, and pour out the vials of the wrath of God upon the earth. And the first went, and poured out his vial upon the earth; and there fell a noisome and grievous sore upon the men which had the mark of the beast, and upon them which worshipped his image. And the second angel poured out his vial upon the sea; and it became as the blood of a dead man: and every living soul died in the sea" (verses 1-3).

"And the third angel poured out his vial upon the rivers and fountains of waters; and they became blood. And I heard the angel of the waters say, Thou art righteous, O Lord, which art, and wast, and shalt be, because thou hast judged thus. For they have shed the blood of saints and prophets, and thou hast given them blood to drink; for they are worthy. And I heard another out of the altar say, Even so, Lord God Almighty, true and righteous are thy judgments" (verses 4-7).

"And the fourth angel poured out his vial upon the sun; and power was given unto him to scorch men with fire. And men were scorched with great heat, and blasphemed the name of God, which hath power over these plagues: and they repented not to give him glory" (verses 8, 9).

"And the fifth angel poured out his vial upon the seat of the beast; and his kingdom was full of darkness; and they gnawed their tongues for pain, And blasphemed the God of heaven because of their pains and their sores, and repented not of their deeds. And the sixth angel poured out his vial upon the great river Euphrates; and the water thereof was dried up, that the way of the kings of the east might be prepared" (verses 10-12).

"And the seventh angel poured out his vial into the air; and there came a great voice out of the temple of heaven, from the throne, saying, It is done. And there were voices, and thunders, and lightnings; and there was a great earthquake, such as was not since men was upon the earth, so mighty an earthquake, and so great. And the great city was divided into three parts, and the cities of the nations fell: and great Babylon came in remembrance before God, to give unto her the cup of the wine of the fierceness of his wrath. And every island fled away, and the mountains were not found. And there fell upon men a great hail out of heaven, every stone about the weight of talent: and men blasphemed God because of the plague of the hail; for the plague thereof was exceeding great" (verses 17-21).

> The seven last plagues is not hell. Hell will not be in this life.

The seven last plagues is not hell. Hell will not be in this life. It will be in the afterlife, a thousand years later. The pouring out of the "seven last plagues" will be simultaneous with the time of trouble. They will immediately follow after judgment has ended. This is the time when history will repeat itself in both cases. While the wicked are experiencing the effects of the plagues, the saints of God will be going through their darkest time in tribulation. How long will this time period last? "For he will finish the work, and cut it short in righteousness: because a short work will the Lord make upon the earth" (Rom. 9:28). Then cometh redemption!

Redemption Draweth Nigh

"Immediately after the tribulation of those days shall the sun be darkened, and the moon shall not give her light, and the stars shall fall from heaven, and the powers of heaven shall be shaken: And then shall appear the sign of the Son of man in heaven: and then shall all the tribes of the earth mourn, and they shall see the Son of man coming in the clouds of heaven with power and great glory" (Matt. 24:29, 30). "And when these things begin to come to pass, then look up, and lift up your heads; for your redemption draweth nigh" (Luke 21:28).

This is the moment we have been waiting for, the most glorious time—the coming of the Savior of the world. This will occur immediately after the time of trouble for God's people has ended. His appearing will be so glorious that the sun and the moon need not give their lights. Matthew 24 describes it as a lightning coming out of the east. It is going to be very bright yet, "every eye shall see him" (Rev. 1:7).

"The powers of heaven shall be shaken" (Luke 21:26) is the same idea that is presented in the sixth seal in Revelation 6:12, which tells us that a great earthquake will come. The prophet Isaiah says that "the earth shall reel to and fro like a drunkard" (Isa. 24:20), while Jeremiah said, "I beheld the mountains, and lo, they trembled, and all the hills moved lightly" (Jer. 4:24). This shaking of the powers of heaven will make all the tribes of the earth mourn.

"For the Lord himself shall descend from heaven with a shout, with the voice of the archangel, and with the trump of God" (1 Thess. 4:16). The Lord God will send His angels with a great sound of trumpets, and they shall gather together His elect from the four comers of the earth, from one end of heaven to the other. His coming will be loud and everyone will hear Him.

> This is the moment we have been waiting for, the most glorious time—the coming of the Savior of the world.

"Then shall two be in the field; the one shall be taken, and the other left. Two women shall be grinding at the mill; the one shall be taken, and the other left" (Matt. 24:40, 41). The angels of God are the ones taking the righteous up to the clouds where the Lord sits, and they are leaving behind the wicked.

The "two" in the field and the "two" women grinding in the mill are parables given to us by Jesus to symbolize sin and righteousness. These two categories were represented by the two thieves on either side of Jesus as He hung on the cross of Calvary. One was saved and the other was not. His coming back to earth is all about salvation and damnation. "For the Son of man shall come in the glory of his Father with his angels; and then he shall reward every man according to his works" (Matt. 16:27). His reward is eternal life to the righteous and eternal damnation to the wicked.

Roadmap to God's Kingdom

The wicked at this point will call for peace and safety, but they will not find it (1 Thess. 5:2, 3). He says in his heart, "My lord delayeth his coming . . . The lord of that servant shall come in a day when he looketh not for him, and in an hour that he is not aware of, And shall cut him asunder, and appoint him his portion with the hypocrites: there shall be weeping and gnashing of teeth" (Matt. 24:48-51). "Watch therefore, for ye know neither the day nor the hour wherein the Son of man cometh" (Matt. 25:13).

> When He comes, the saints will come running out into the open with hands held high, rejoicing to see Jesus Christ, their Lord and Savior.

The apostle John describes the wicked in Revelation 6:15-17: "And the kings of the earth, and the great men, and the rich men, and the chief captains, and the mighty men, and every bondmen, and every free man, hid themselves in the dens and in the rocks of the mountains; And said to the mountains and rocks, Fall on us, and hide us from the face of him that sitteth on the throne, and from the wrath of the Lamb. For the great day of his wrath is come; and who shall be able to stand?"

In the writings of the apostle Paul, he says, "And then shall that Wicked be revealed, whom the Lord shall consume with the spirit of his mouth, and shall destroy with the brightness of his coming" (2 Thess. 2:8). "In flaming fire taking vengeance on them that know not God, and obey not the gospel of our Lord Jesus Christ: Who shall be punished with everlasting destruction from the presence of the Lord, and from the glory of his power" (2 Thess. 1:8, 9). The wicked shall be "consumed and destroyed" when He comes.

42

The righteous will come out of the rocks, out of the cave, and down from the fortress of the mountains to meet their Lord and Savior. During the time of trouble, the Lord will have sent His angels to hide them: "For in the time of trouble he shall hide me in his pavilion: in the secret of his tabernacle shall he hide me; he shall set me up upon a rock" (Ps. 27:5).

Isaiah 26:20 says, "Come, my people, enter thou into thy chambers, and shut thy doors about thee: hide thyself as it were for a little moment, until the indignation be overpast." God will take care of his own in this period of indignation: "Bread shall be given him; his waters shall be sure" (Isa. 33:16).

When He comes, the saints will come running out into the open with hands held high, rejoicing to see Jesus Christ, their Lord and Savior. They will come out from the four corners of the earth with beaming faces, and cry; "Lo, this is our God; we have waited for him, and he will save us" (Isa. 25:9). Suddenly, an angel of God comes around and takes them up to Jesus. Oh, what a glorious day that will be. The righteous in the graves will be resurrected. When they do, they will look beautiful and heavenly. Their bodies will be changed from mortal to immortal (1 Cor. 15:51-55). They will be taken up in the clouds to where the Savior waits, and they shall reign with him a thousand years. They shall ever be with the Lord (1 Thess. 4:17).

"And I saw as it were a sea of glass mingled with fire: and them that had gotten the victory over the beast, and over his image, and over his mark, and over the number of his name, stand on the sea of glass, having the harps of God. And they sing the song of Moses the servant of God, and the song of the Lamb, saying, Great and marvellous are thy works, Lord God Almighty; just and true are thy ways, thou King of saints" (Rev. 15:2, 3).

These are also the saints of God described in Revelation 7:9-15. They are a great multitude, which no man can number, of all nations, and kindred, and people, and tongues, standing before the throne and the Lamb, clothed with white robes, and palms in their hands. This great multitude is outside of the one hundred forty and four thousand. They too came out of the great tribulation and have washed their robes and have made them white in the blood of the Lamb.

> The redemption of God's saints on earth in His soon appearing will complete the second half of the plan of redemption.

"Wash their robes" means that they are sanctified by God. They have confessed and repented of their sins to a gracious God, and they have been forgiven. The redemption of God's saints on earth in His soon appearing will complete the second half of the plan of redemption. The first half was done on the cross of Calvary, when he died for the sins of the world some two thousand years ago. Thus, the plan is fulfilled: "For God so love the world, that he gave his only begotten Son, that whosoever believeth in him should not perish, but have everlasting life" (John 3:16). The Scriptures describe that He will come "once" in this life to gather His own, and then, He will return with the saints in the "New Jerusalem" after the one thousand years.

Yes, there will be a New Jerusalem, but this New Jerusalem will be built in heaven and not on this earth. God will build it Himself: "And I John saw the holy city, new Jerusalem, coming down from God out of heaven" (Rev. 21:2). A detailed description of this city is given in the new chapter.

The One Thousand Years

The earth is now very quiet. The saints are gone. They went to reign with God for a thousand years. What is left behind are the wicked, but they are all dead. There was a resurrection when the Lord came, but that was only for the righteous; the wicked remained dead (Rev. 20:5, 6). There were those who were alive when He came, but they all died (2 Thess. 2:8).

The high-rise buildings that once stood are now rubble. The beautiful apartments, houses, condominiums, and mansions that were once haven to its residents are all broken down to the ground. No structure ever built by men withstood the destruction from the presence of the Lord when the powers of heaven were shaken. Even the mountains and the rocks fell. The islands disappeared. The earth is in absolute devastation. It is totally desolated. There is no sign of life anywhere (Rev. 6:12-14).

But Satan and his angels are here. This will be their home for a thousand years. It is a "bottomless pit." It is an endless space of nothing. It is like he and his angels are chained to it (Rev. 20:1-3). They will not be able to go anywhere even if they wanted. The bad part about this is that they thrive on deceiving people, and there is no one else to deceive. There is no soul that is alive. Everyone is dead. He was out to "deceive the world," but the world he went to deceive ended when the Lord came. Everyone he had deceived are dead. Except for the wind that blows, the whole earth is still and silent and will remain so until the one thousand years are finished.

The New Jerusalem

"And I saw a new heaven and a new earth: for the first heaven and the first earth were passed away; and there was no more sea. And I John saw the holy city, new Jerusalem, coming down from God out of heaven, prepared as a bride adorned for her husband. And I heard a voice out of heaven saying, Behold, the tabernacle of God is with men, and he will dwell with them, and they shall be his people, and God himself shall be with them, and be their God. And God shall wipe away all tears from their eyes, and there shall be no more death, neither sorrow, nor crying, neither shall there be any more pain: for the former things are passed away" (Rev. 21:1-4).

The "people" referred to here, shown to John in a vision, are the saints that were redeemed from the earth. They were in heaven with the Lord. They reigned with Him there for a thousand years. The reason He did not set his foot on earth when He came was that He was going straight back to heaven with the saints. Jesus sat in the clouds and sent His holy angels to gather the saints from the four corners of the earth; then He went straight back to heaven.

John said, "And there came unto me one of the seven angels which had the seven vials full of the seven last plagues, and talked with me, saying, Come hither, I will shew thee the bride, the Lamb's wife. And he carried me away in the spirit to a great and high mountain, and shewed me that great city, the holy Jerusalem, descending out of heaven from God" (Rev. 21:9, 10).

"Having the glory of God: and her light was like unto a stone most precious, even like a jasper stone, clear as crystal; And had a wall great and high, and had twelve gates, and at the gate twelve angels, and names written thereon, which are the names of the twelve tribes of the children of Israel: On the east three gates; on the north three gates; on the south three gates; and on the west three gates. And the wall of the city had twelve foundations, and in them the names of the twelve apostles of the Lamb" (verses 11-14).

> The commandments of God are essential to the lives of the saints on earth while preparing for His kingdom. It shows their allegiance and respect to the creator of heaven and earth.

"And the city lieth foursquare, and the length is as large as the breadth: and he measured the city with the reed, twelve thousand furlongs. The length and the breadth and the height of it are equal. And he measured the wall thereof, an hundred and forty and four cubits, according to the measure of a man, that is, of the angel. And the building of the wall of it was of jasper: and the city was pure gold, like unto clear glass. . . . And the twelve gates were twelve pearls: every several gate was of one pearl: and the street of the city was pure gold, as it were transparent glass" (verses 16-21).

48

"And I saw no temple therein: for the Lord God Almighty and the Lamb are the temple of it. And the city had no need of the sun, neither of the moon, to shine in it: for the glory of God did lighten it, and the Lamb is the light thereof. . . . And the gates of it shall not be shut at all by day: for there shall be no night there. . . . And there shall in no wise enter into it any thing that defileth, neither whatsoever worketh abomination, or maketh a lie: but they which are written in the Lamb's book of life" (verses 22-27).

"And he shewed me a pure river of water of life, clear as crystal, proceeding out of the throne of God and of the Lamb. In the midst of the street of it, and on either side of the river, was there the tree of life, which bare twelve manner of fruits, and yielded her fruit every month: and the leaves of the tree were for healing of the nations" (Rev. 22:1, 2). "Blessed are they that do his commandments, that they may have the right to the tree of life, and may enter in through the gates into the city" (verse 14).

The commandments of God are essential to the lives of the saints on earth while preparing for His kingdom. It shows their allegiance and respect to the creator of heaven and earth. David, the psalmist, says, "Thy word is a lamp unto my feet, and a light unto my path" (Ps. 119:105). It lightens our path and shows us the way. In the New Jerusalem, His laws will be inherent. "This is the covenant that I will make with them after those days, saith the Lord, I will put my laws into their hearts, and in their minds will I write them; And their sins and iniquities will I remember no more" (Heb. 10:16, 17).

Armageddon

"And when the thousand years are expired, Satan shall be loosed out of his prison" (Rev. 20:7). What is he going to do at that time? "And [he] shall go out to deceive the nations which are in the four quarters of the earth, Gog, and Magog, to gather them together to battle: the number of whom is as the sand of the sea" (verse 8).

Who are these "nations" he is going to deceive? In the fifth verse of the same chapter, it says, "But the rest of the dead lived not again until the thousand years were finished." This is the "second resurrection," and these are the wicked that Satan is going to deceive again after the one thousand years.

When the righteous were resurrected a thousand years earlier, they were changed from their sinful, wicked, and mortal bodies to a beautiful, heavenly, and immortal state—like the angels of God. Whereas the wicked will be resurrected in the same condition they were when they died. The "marks of curse" will be visible upon them. No change for the better whatsoever. This will be their "life after death" experience, and it will be brief. They are alive to participate in the Armageddon.

Satan and his angels have always tried to challenge God in every way possible, since day one of his existence. Satan tried to amend God's laws. In heaven, Lucifer wanted to "ascend above the heights of the clouds; I will be like the most High" (Isa. 14:14). He has circumvented God's words and laws in so many ways. "Woe to the inhabiters of the earth and of the sea! for the devil is come down unto you, having great wrath, because he knoweth that he hath but a short time" (Rev. 12:12).

Armageddon will be the biggest, fiercest, and most damaging war that will ever occur between the forces of evil and the heavenly host. It will be the final conflict between Christ and Satan. It will be attended and participated by everyone who had the mark of the beast and those who will wake up to the resurrection of "everlasting contempt" (Dan. 12:2). It will take place in the valley of Megiddo, not far from the gates of the holy city of God.

> Armageddon will be the biggest, fiercest, and most damaging war that will ever occur between the forces of evil and the heavenly host.

The New Jerusalem has come down from God out of heaven. The wicked are resurrected. Satan and his angels are now free to deceive the nations once more and gather them together to battle God. Satan himself, the great deceiver, will be in charge. The beast of Revelation 13 will no longer be in power, but he will be there with the false prophets.

They are "numberless." Those whom the devil has deceived are like the sands of the sea. Remember the wide gate? These are those who were proud and rebellious of God's words and laws. They were defiant, disobedient unbelievers, and they would not confess and repent of their misdeeds. Some of these people are best described in Matthew 7:21-23. They were Christians. They went to church. They carried their Bibles to church, but they would rather follow the changes made by the beast, instead of adhering to God's words and laws. This time it's a little bit too late. Judgment has ended, the two gates are closed, and there is no more turning back. God's mercy has ended.

"And they went up on the breadth of the earth, and compassed the camp of the saints about, and the beloved city [the New Jerusalem]: and fire came down from God out of heaven, and devoured them. And the devil that deceived them was cast into the lake of fire and brimstone, where the beast and the false prophets are, and shall be tormented day and night for ever and ever" (Rev. 20:9, 10). "And death and hell were cast into the lake of fire. This is the second death. And whosoever was not found written in the book of life was cast into the lake of fire" (verses 14, 15). "The fearful, and unbelieving, and the abominable, and murderers, and whoremongers, and sorcerers, and idolaters, and all liars, shall have their part in the lake which burneth with fire and brimstone: which is the second death" (Rev. 21:8).

This is the penalty phase of the judgment for the wicked—hell! It is Armageddon!

Eternity Begins

The thousand years have expired. The New Jerusalem has come down and settled on the mount of Olives (Zech. 14:4, 5). The final conflict between Christ and Satan is over. The earth has been cleansed from sin. It is now "the earth made new." It is here that the Lord will reign with the saints. It is here where eternity begins. "Blessed are the meek: for they shall inherit the earth" (Matt. 5:5).

There is no more pain, no more sorrow, no more tears, and no more death (Rev. 21:4). There is no more swine flu, no cancer, and no heart disease. Unemployment, foreclosures, and recession will be things of the past and will not be remembered anymore. Devastation from wild fires, floods, tornadoes, and earthquakes are non-existent. No more Wall Street crashes, no more CEO bonuses, and no more stimulus packages.

It's peaceful here. There is no more sin, and there are no more sinners. Satan and his angels are gone. The beast and the false prophets perished in hell with the deceived. It is the new heaven and new earth. The prophet Isaiah says, "For, behold, I create new heavens and a new earth: and the former shall not be remembered, nor come into mind. But be ye glad and rejoice for ever in that which I create: for, behold, I create Jerusalem a rejoicing, and her people a joy" (Isa. 65:17, 18).

The final conflict between Christ and Satan is over. The earth has been cleansed from sin. It is now "the earth made new."

"And they shall build houses, and inhabit them; and they shall plant vineyards, and eat the fruit of them. They shall not build, and another inhabit; they shall not plant, and another eat" (verses 21, 22). "And it shall come to pass, that before they call, I will answer; and while they are yet speaking, I will hear. The wolf and the lamb shall feed together, and the lion shall eat straw like the bullock: and dust shall be the serpent's meat. They shall not hurt nor destroy in my holy mountain, saith the Lord" (verses 24, 25).

"For as the new heavens and the new earth, which I will make, shall remain before me, saith the LORD, so shall your seed and your name remain. And it shall come to pass, that from one new moon to another, and from one sabbath to another, shall all flesh come to worship before me, saith the LORD" (Isa. 66:22, 23).

The "seventh day is the sabbath of the LORD thy God" (Ex. 20:10), and it will continue to be revered and observed by the saints in the new heaven and new earth. It was never changed by God, and it will continue to be followed throughout the ages of eternity and beyond.

We invite you to view the complete
selection of titles we publish at:

www.LNFBooks.com

or write or email us your praises,
reactions, or thoughts about this
or any other book we publish at:

TEACH Services, Inc.
P.O. Box 954
Ringgold, GA 30736

info@TEACHServices.com

* 9 7 8 1 5 7 2 5 8 6 3 4 5 *